Hanna Y

ALL ABOUT BODY SAFETY

My Guide to Keep Body Safe!

NOTE FOR PARENTS

Body safety is a very important and critical topic to start a conversation with your child. It is essential for parents to build a strong relationship with their kids and give them the space to discuss these complex but important issues.

For a child to be able to confide in you and feel safe to initiate this conversation, they must have a good relationship with their parents. It can be achieved by taking elementary steps - giving them time during the day or bedtime and making it a routine to give age-appropriate information in small chunks.

NOTE FOR PARENTS

Teaching children about body safety not only helps them to protect themselves but also to be more empathic and respectful towards others. It also helps to prevent abuse and inappropriate behavior. By having open and age-appropriate conversations with your child about body safety, you are equipping them with the tools they need to navigate the world safely and confidently.

I hope that this book will start important conversations with your child and empower them to understand and respect their own and others' body boundaries.

THIS BOOK BELONGS TO

WHAT IS BODY SAFETY?

BODY SAFETY IS ABOUT TAKING CARE OF OURSELVES AND PROTECTING OURSELVES FROM ANY HARM.

NO ONE HAS THE RIGHT TO HURT ME OR
TOUCH ME WITHOUT MY PERMISSION.

LIKE EVERY OTHER CHILD, I HAVE THE RIGHT TO FEEL SAFE AND RESPECTED IN MY OWN BODY.

WHAT IS MY PERSONAL SPACE? SAFETY CIRCLE" OR "PROTECTIVE CIRCLE

PERSONAL SPACE IS LIKE HAVING A "BUBBLE" AROUND ME. IT'S A SPACE THAT BELONGS TO ME AND I GET TO DECIDE WHO CAN COME INTO MY BUBBLE AND WHO CAN'T.

EVERYONE HAS THE RIGHT TO THEIR OWN SPACE, AND SO DO I. NO ONE SHOULD INVADE MY PERSONAL SPACE WITHOUT MY PERMISSION.

RESPECT OTHER PEOPLE'S PERSONAL SPACE AND ALWAYS ASK FOR PERMISSION BEFORE HUGGING OR TOUCHING.

PRIVATE PARTS ARE PRIVATE

PRIVATE BODY PARTS

CERTAIN PARTS OF OUR BODY ARE
PRIVATE AND SHOULD NOT BE TOUCHED
BY OTHERS.

MY PRIVATE PARTS BELONG TO ME

NO ONE HAS THE RIGHT TO TOUCH MY PRIVATE PARTS.

MY PRIVATE PARTS BELONG TO ME

MY PRIVATE PARTS ARE SPECIAL AND

SHOULD ONLY BE TOUCHED BY MYSELF.

(CHEST AND PARTS OF THE BODY

COVERED BY UNDERWEAR)

IF AND WHEN NECESSARY, MY PRIVATE BODY PARTS CAN BE TOUCHED DURING A MEDICAL OR HYGIENE CHECK-UP.

CAN YOU NAME YOUR BODY PARTS?

CAN YOU NAME YOUR BODY PARTS?

GOOD TOUCH
Vs
BAD TOUCH

GOOD TOUCH IS THAT WHICH IS APPROPRIATE AND CONSENSUAL. FOR EXAMPLE, HUG FROM A TRUSTED ADULT OR HIGH FIVE FROM A FRIEND IS A GOOD TOUCH.

GOOD TOUCH

GOOD TOUCH

BAD TOUCH IS THAT WHICH IS NOT APPROPRIATE AND WITHOUT CONSENT.

BAD TOUCH

BAD TOUCH

FOR EXAMPLE, SOMEONE TOUCHING ME IN A WAY THAT MAKES ME UNCOMFORTABLE BY TOUCHING MY LIPS OR OTHER PRIVATE PARTS.

BAD TOUCH

BAD TOUCH

BAD TOUCH IS WHEN A RELATIVE IS
TRYING TO HUG OR KISS ME WHEN I
DON'T WANT TO.

BAD TOUCH

A STRANGER ASKING TO COME CLOSER OR TOUCH MY BODY PARTS IS A BAD TOUCH.

BAD TOUCH

BAD TOUCH IS WHEN A FRIEND IS TRYING TO TICKLE ME EVEN WHEN I SAY STOP.

SAY NO TO UNWANTED TOUCHES

WE SHOULD ALWAYS TELL A TRUSTED ADULT IF SOMEONE TRIES TO TOUCH OUR PRIVATE PARTS.

WHO ARE TRUSTED ADULTS?

TRUSTED ADULTS ARE THOSE PEOPLE WHO I CAN TALK TO AND GO FOR HELP IF I FEEL UNSAFE OR UNCOMFORTABLE.

THESE ARE EXAMPLES OF TRUSTED ADULTS. PARENTS, TEACHERS, DOCTORS, AND GRAND PARENTS

SAYING NO

I SHOULD SPEAK UP FOR MYSELF AND SAY NO IF SOMEONE TRIES TO TOUCH MY BODY PARTS IN A WAY THAT MAKES ME UNSAFE OR UNCOMFORTABLE.

I SAY NO IN A CONFIDENT AND STRONG VOICE, AND I REMOVE MYSELF FROM THE UNSAFE SITUATION.

I ALWAYS TRUST MY INSTINCT AND SPEAK UP IF I FEEL UNSAFE.

MY BODY BELONGS TO ME

I HAVE THE RIGHT TO SAY NO TO PHYSICAL CONTACT THAT MAKES ME FEEL UNCOMFORTABLE.

I CAN TALK ABOUT MY FEELINGS

IT IS OK TO EXPRESS MY FEELINGS AND TALK TO TRUSTED ADULTS ABOUT MY FEELINGS.

SECRET TOUCHES

NEVER KEEP SECRETS ABOUT BAD TOUCHES EVEN IF SOMEONE SAYS TO KEEP SECRETS AFTER BAD TOUCHES.

ASK FOR HELP

I TRUST MY INSTINCTS AND SEEK HELP FROM A TRUSTED ADULT IF SOMEONE TOUCHES ME IN AN UNSAFE AND UNCOMFORTABLE MANNER.

TRUSTED ADULTS ARE PEOPLE SUCH AS PARENTS, AND TEACHERS

BE A GOOD FRIEND

I SHOULD BE SUPPORTIVE AND STAND
UP FOR MY FRIENDS.

IF I SEE SOMEONE ELSE TOUCHING
THEIR BODY IN AN UNSAFE AND
INAPPROPRIATE MANNER.

I MUST SEEK HELP FROM A TRUSTED
ADULT.

IMPORTANT LESSONS

- I SHOULD KNOW MY PRIVATE BODY PARTS

- I SHOULD BE ABLE TO COMMUNICATE WITH TRUSTED ADULTS IF SOMEONE TOUCHES MY PRIVATE PARTS INAPPROPRIATELY

- MY PRIVATE PARTS ARE PRIVATE. THEY ARE NOT FOR EVERYONE ELSE TO TOUCH OR SEE

- ONLY TRUSTED INDIVIDUALS CAN SEE OR TOUCH MY PRIVATE PARTS IF NEEDED FOR EXAMPLE DURING NECESSARY MEDICAL EXAMINATIONS AND HYGIENE ROUTINES

- I SHOULD BE ABLE TO SAY NO IF SOMEONE TOUCHES MY PRIVATE BODY PARTS INAPPROPRIATELY AND WITHOUT MY CONSENT

- I SHOULD ASK FOR HELP FROM A TRUSTED ADULT IF I FEEL UNSAFE AND UNCOMFORTABLE

- I SHOULD BE A GOOD FRIEND AND RESPECT OTHER PEOPLE'S BOUNDARIES

- I SHOULD BE SUPPORTIVE AND STAND UP FOR MY FRIENDS IF I SEE SOMEONE INVADING THEIR BODY SAFETY BOUNDARIES

REMEMBER, BODY SAFETY IS SO IMPORTANT!

IT IS OKAY TO SPEAK UP AND ASK FOR HELP IF WE EVER FEEL UNSAFE.

LET US ALWAYS TAKE CARE OF OURSELVES AND PROTECT OUR BODIES.

Author's note:

Thank you so much for reading this book. Once you read this book, I want your honest review and feedback so that I can improve the book. I take all the reviews and feedback seriously and will try my best to make this book even better.

Please consider leaving a review on Amazon. CLICK HERE to leave a review on Amazon.

Thank you for your support!
- Hanna Yameen

Scan the QR code below to give feedback!

Made in the USA
Columbia, SC
17 June 2025

59495957R10027